What shall I make?

Ray Gibson
Designed by Amanda Barlow

Ilustrated by Chris Chaisty
Photographs by Howard Allman
Edited By Fiona Watt
Series Editor: Jenny Tyler

Contents

Make a talking bird

1. Fold three paper plates in half. Then, bend each one back along the fold.

2. Cut one plate along the fold. Cut a strip from the edge of one half.

You don't need these.

3. Mix household glue (PVA) with red, orange and yellow paint. Paint the plates like this.

4. When the paint has dried, put the two whole plates together like this.

  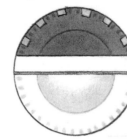

5. Tape the orange and red parts together around the edge.

6. Turn it over and tape the orange piece onto the red half.

7. Make a roll of crêpe paper. Cut lots of slits in it.

8. Tape the paper onto the back of the yellow part.

9. Glue on paper eyes. You could glue on buttons for the middles.

You could add bright feathers instead of paper to the bird's head.

10. Cut a hole in a sock for your thumb and put your hand inside.

11. Put your hand into the bird. Open and close your hand to make it talk.

Make a wobbling head

   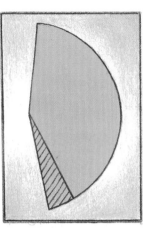

1. Paint a clean eggshell. Dry it upside down. Roll a ball of model dough the size of a marble.

2. Wet a finger and rub it on one side of the model dough. Press it into the bottom of the egg.

3. Cut lots of pieces of yarn for hair. Glue them around the top of the eggshell.

4. Put tracing paper over the pattern for the hat on page 32. Draw over the lines carefully.

Sprinkle glitter onto dots of glue.

Add a pair of glasses and a gift wrap hat.

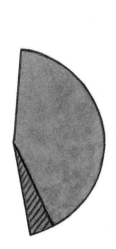
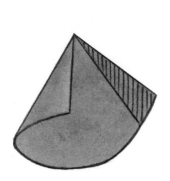

5. Glue the tracing paper onto bright paper with a glue stick. Cut around the shape.

6. Put glue on the shaded part of the pattern. Overlap the sides. Press them together.

7. Glue around the inside edge of the hat. Push the hat over the hair onto the head.

8. Paint a nose and a smiling mouth. Add middles to the eyes in a different shade.

Add lots of shapes all over the hat.

Cut a crown from shiny paper.

Make a parachute

1. Cut one side from a plastic carrier bag. Lay it flat.

2. Lay this book on top. Draw around it with a pen.

3. Cut it out. Fold over the top corner like this. Draw a line.

4. Fold the corner back up and cut along the line.

5. Poke a hole in each corner with a ballpoint pen.

6. Cut four pieces of thread as long as this book.

7. Poke one piece through one of the holes. Tie a knot.

8. Do the same with the other three corners.

9. Bring all the ends together. Tie them in a big knot.

10. Tape the knot to the back of a small model.

Fly your
parachute
outside. Crumple
it in your hand.
Put the model on
top and throw them
high into the air.

7

Make a furry snake

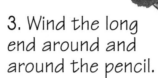

1. For the head,
bend over one end
of a pipecleaner.

2. Put it along a
pencil and bend the
head over the end.

3. Wind the long
end around and
around the pencil.

4. Gently pull the
snake halfway off
the pencil.

5. Cut some paper
eyes and glue them
onto the head.

6. Draw a red
tongue. Cut it out
and glue it on.

Make some bangles

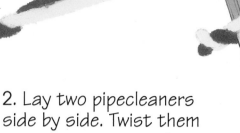

1. Take two pencils and tape them together like this.

2. Lay two pipecleaners side by side. Twist them together at one end.

3. Put the pencils between the pipecleaners, close to the twisted part.

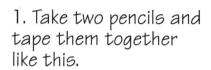

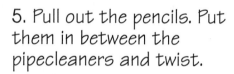

4. Twist the pipecleaners tightly next to the pencils, three times.

5. Pull out the pencils. Put them in between the pipecleaners and twist.

6. Keep on doing this to the end. Press the twisted pipecleaners flat.

7. Bend them into a circle. Twist the ends together.

Make a mask

1. Take some stiff paper as big as this book. Fold it in half, short sides together.

2. Put some sunglasses along the bottom, halfway across the fold.

3. Draw around the shape. Add an eye, then poke a hole in it with a pencil.

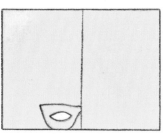

4. Push scissors into the hole. Cut to the edge of the eye, then cut it out.

Glue on shiny shapes and sequins.

5. Fold the paper again. Draw around the eye shape onto the paper below.

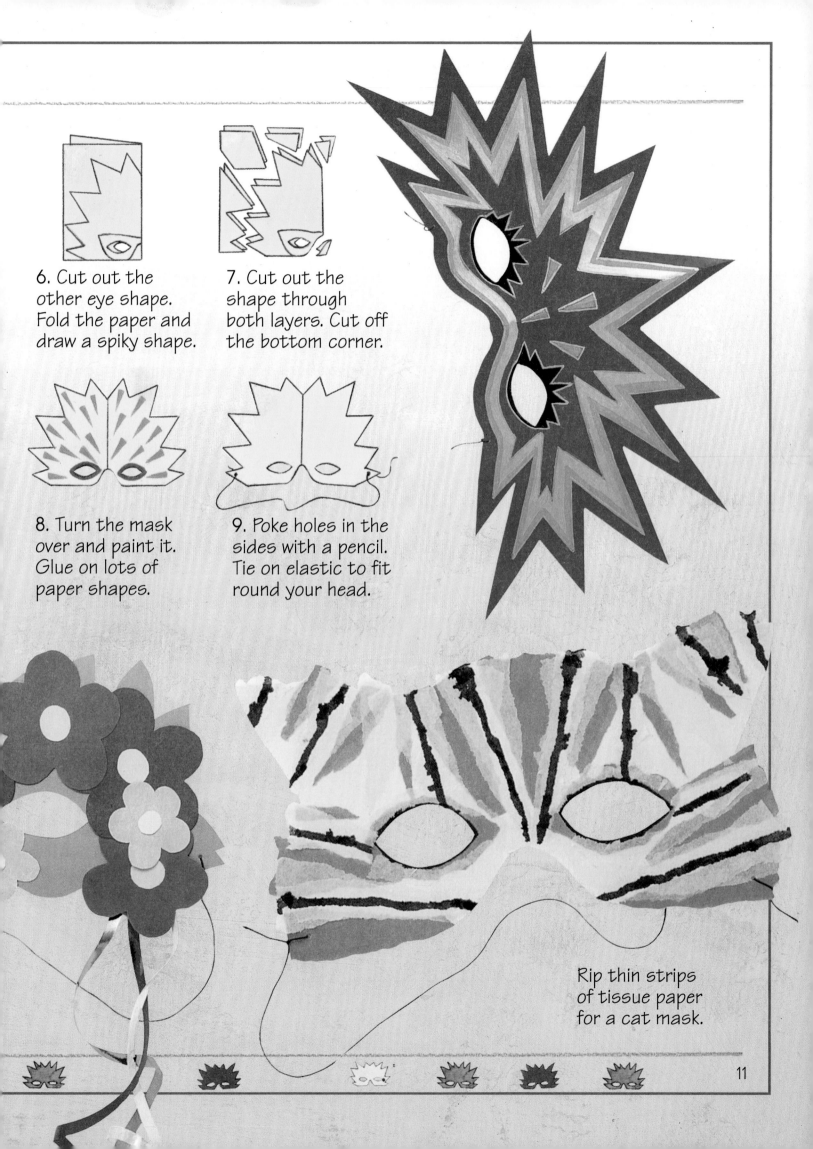

6. Cut out the other eye shape. Fold the paper and draw a spiky shape.

7. Cut out the shape through both layers. Cut off the bottom corner.

8. Turn the mask over and paint it. Glue on lots of paper shapes.

9. Poke holes in the sides with a pencil. Tie on elastic to fit round your head.

Rip thin strips of tissue paper for a cat mask.

Make some vegetable people

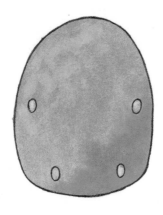

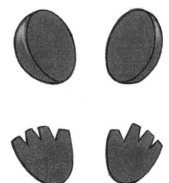

1. Wash and dry a large potato. Cut a slice off one end so that it stands up.

2. Poke four holes in the front of the potato with a sharp pencil.

3. Cut two pipecleaners in half. Push a piece into each hole.

4. Make hands and feet from small balls of playdough.

5. Press the hands and feet onto the ends of the pipecleaners.

6. Make a face by adding a round nose and a smiling mouth.

7. Press on two circles for eyes. Add smaller middles to them.

8. Press model dough through a sieve and scrape it off with a knife. Press it on.

A flower hat

Ball of model dough

Flat model dough

Strip of model dough

Push the ball onto the flat piece. Roll up lots of strips to make flowers. Press them on.

A tall hat

Roll of model dough

Circle of model dough

Add a band.

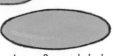

A bag

Squashed ball of model dough

Add a handle.

Add a clip.

You can make
people from
all types of
vegetables.

Make bread shapes

These bread shapes are decorations only. Do not eat them.

1. Press a big cookie cutter firmly into a slice of white bread.

2. Push the shape gently out of the cutter.

3. Make a hole by pressing the end of a straw into the shape.

4. Put it onto a baking rack and leave it overnight to go hard.

5. Mix a little paint with household glue (PVA). Paint the edges of the shape.

6. Paint the top. When it is dry, turn it over and paint the other side.

7. Glue on lots of glitter, sequins or beads to decorate your shape.

8. Push thread through the hole. Bring the ends together to make a loop.

9. Push the ends of the thread through the loop to make a knot.

Make paper flowers

A daisy

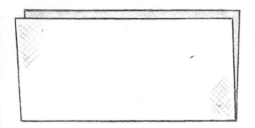

1. Fold a sheet of kitchen paper towel in half. Open it out. Cut along the fold.

2. Fold one piece in half, long sides together. You don't need the other piece.

3. Draw lots of stripes along the paper with a felt-tip pen.

4. Fold in half with the short sides together, then fold it in half again.

5. Make long cuts close together from the bottom. Don't cut all the way up.

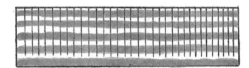

6. Open it carefully, so that it looks like this.

7. Tape one end of the paper onto a bendable straw. Roll the paper tightly around it.

8. Fasten the loose end with tape. Pull all the petals down.

9. Snip little pieces of yellow paper or yarn. Glue them into the middle.

You can use tissue paper for bright flowers. Cut the paper the same size as a piece of paper towel.

Another flower

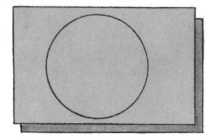  

1. Take two sheets of tissue paper. Put a small plate or saucer on top and draw around it.

2. Cut around the circle through both layers of tissue paper. Fold them in half and in half again.

3. Twist the corner and tape onto the end of a straw. Gently pull the petals apart.

4. Make a ball of tissue paper and glue it in the middle.

Make a fish

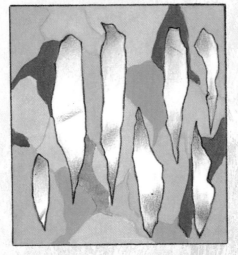

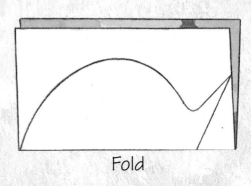

Fold

1. Fold a piece of paper in half, long sides together. Open it. Crease it back along the same fold.

2. Open the paper. Tear pieces of tissue paper. Glue them on. Add lots of strips of kitchen foil.

3. Fold the paper in half. Crease the fold well. Draw half a fat fish shape. Cut it out.

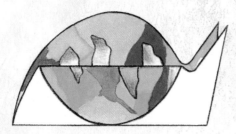

Mouth

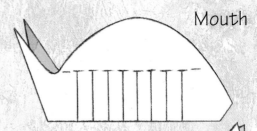

4. Bend over one of the top edges until it touches the fold at the bottom. Press hard to crease it.

5. Turn the fish over. Bend the other top edge over in the same way. Remember to crease it well.

6. Unfold the top pieces. Snip a mouth. Make cuts as wide as your finger, up to the fold.

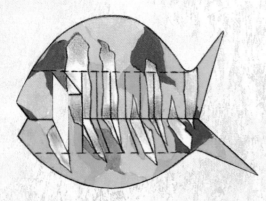

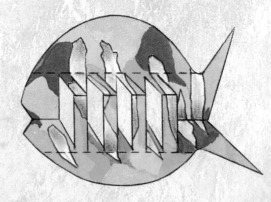

7. Half open the fish. Hold the head and pull the first strip out. Pinch the fold in the middle so that it stands up.

8. Skip the next strip. Pull out the next one. Go on in the same way until you reach the last strip. Pinch all the folds well.

Use bright
thread to
hang up
your fish.

Make model dough babies

 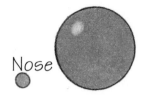    

Nose

1. Make a ball of pink and yellow model dough, the size shown here. Roll them together.

2. Break off a tiny piece and roll the rest back into a ball. Press on the nose.

3. Press in eyes with a pencil. Press a mouth with the end of a straw.

4. Make a ball this size. Use a round pencil like a rolling pin to make it flat.

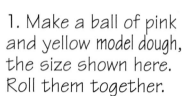 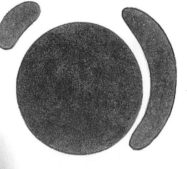    

5. Turn a mug upside down and press it on. Peel away the spare model dough.

6. Press a pencil point around the edge to make it lacy. Turn it over.

7. Put the head near the top. Press on a sausage shape for the body.

8. Wrap one side around the body, then wrap the other side over the top.

9. Gently press the blanket around the baby's head and neck.

Make an octopus

1. Roll a model dough
sausage. Flatten it.
Roll balls for eyes
and press them on.

2. Push a pencil
point into each eye.
Make a mouth with
the end of a spoon.

3. Use scissors
to snip eight
tentacles. Bend
up the side ones.

4. Press the end of
a straw into the
legs, to make
lots of suckers.

5. Make seaweed
from strips of
green model dough.
Cut out some fish.

Make a row of clowns

1. Put tracing paper over the clown pattern on page 32. Draw over the black lines.

2. Draw around all the red lines with a red pencil. Take the paper off.

3. Carefully cut around the black lines, but don't cut out the clown.

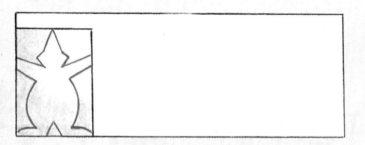

4. Glue the tracing onto the corner of a long sheet of stiff paper.

5. Turn the paper over. Fold the clown to the front. Crease along the edge.

6. Turn the paper over again. Neatly fold the clown back to the front.

7. Turn it over. Fold it to the front again. Cut off the extra paper at the top and side.

8. Cut out the clown along the red lines. Don't cut the black lines at the edges.

9. Pull the clowns open, so that the tracing is on the back. Draw their hats.

10. Draw the clowns' faces. Use paint or felt-tip pens to decorate their clothes.

Make a crown

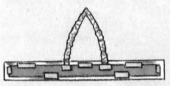

1. Cut a band of
stiff paper to fit
around your head,
plus a little bit.

2. Lay it on a bigger
piece of kitchen foil.
Fold the edges in
and tape them down.

3. Cut four strips of
foil as wide as the
band. Squeeze them
to make thin sticks.

4. Bend one in half.
Tape it onto the
middle of the band,
at the back.

5. Cut a little from
the end of two
pieces. Bend them
and tape them on.

6. Cut the last
piece in half. Bend
each piece. Tape
them on at each end.

7. Cut shiny shapes.
Tape them on so
you can see them
above the band.

8. Turn the band
over. Glue on
scraps of bright
paper or foil.

For an icy
crown, use
only blue and
silver paper.

Make a
smaller
crown for a
ballerina.

9. Tape the ends of the crown together to fit around your head.

For a king's crown, add shapes cut from shiny paper. Add spots with a felt-tip pen for a fur effect.

Make a lacy card

1. Draw some leaves, flowers and hearts on thick white paper.

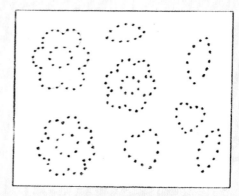

2. Wrap sticky tape around the end of a darning needle to make a handle. Lay several kitchen paper towels over a folded newspaper. Put your drawing on top.

3. Use the needle to prick around the shapes. Press quite hard.

4. Cut around all the shapes very carefully. Leave a narrow edge around the holes.

5. Dab glue stick on the pencil side of each shape. Press them very gently onto thin cardboard.

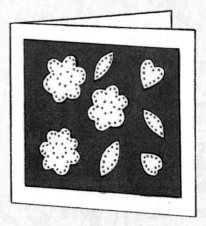

6. To make a card, glue your picture onto a slightly bigger piece of folded cardboard.

Make stamps

Draw a stamp and prick around the edges. Tear it carefully along the holes.

You don't need to use white paper for all your shapes.

Prick a wavy line around your shape Cut around it, but leave a narrow edge.

Make a caterpillar

1. Put this book onto a piece of bright paper. Draw around it and cut it out.

2. Fold it in half. Cut along the fold. Sponge different paint on both sides of one piece.

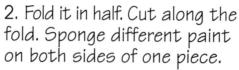

3. Fold the paper in half and in half again. Open it and cut along all the folds.

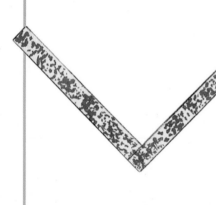

4. Put some glue at the end of one strip and join it to another one like this.

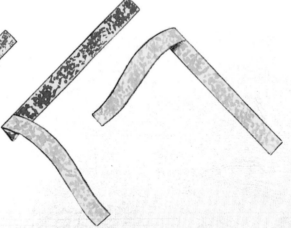

5. Fold the left strip over and crease it. Fold the other strip down over it.

6. Keep folding one strip over the other one to make a concertina shape.

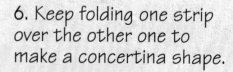

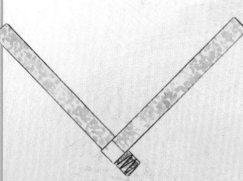

7. When you get near to the end of the strips, glue on the spare strips, then keep on folding.

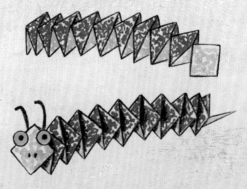

8. When you reach the end glue down the top piece. Trim the ends. Add eyes, feelers and a tail.

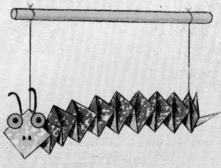

9. Tape some thin elastic behind the head and the tail. Tie the caterpillar onto a straw.

Make a brooch

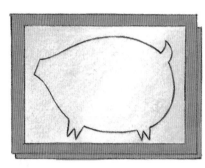

1. Put tracing paper over the pig pattern on page 32. Draw around the shape.

2. Put two pieces of felt together. Pin the tracing paper pattern on top.

3. Cut around the shape. Ask for help for the tricky parts. Take out the pins.

4. Cut the tail from one pig. Trace the pig's ear on page 32. Cut one out from felt.

5. Pin the pigs together. Sew around them with big stitches. Take out the pins.

6. Now sew close to the edge with tiny stitches. Leave a gap at the bottom.

Draw stripes on with a pen.

Glue sequins and beads onto your brooch.

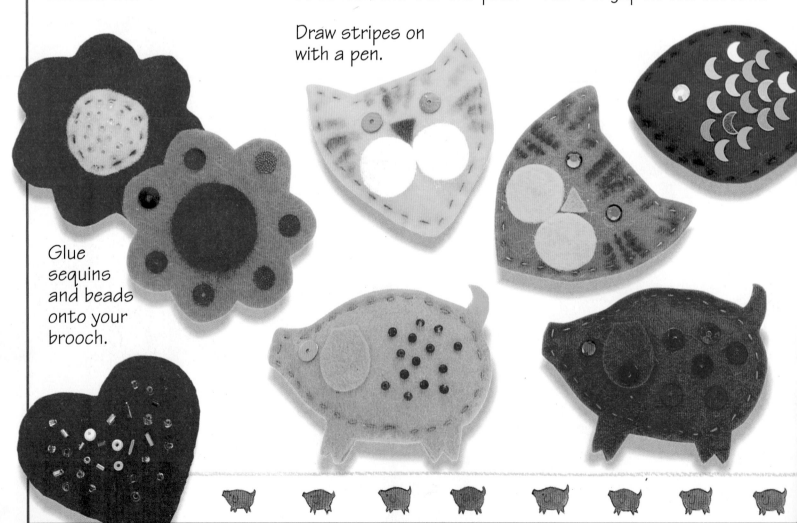

7. Take out the big stitches. Carefully push some stuffing into the hole.

8. Sew up the hole. Glue on the ear. Draw an eye with a felt-tip pen.

9. Turn the pig over. Sew a safety pin onto the back of the brooch.

The patterns for the other brooches shown here are on page 32.

Patterns

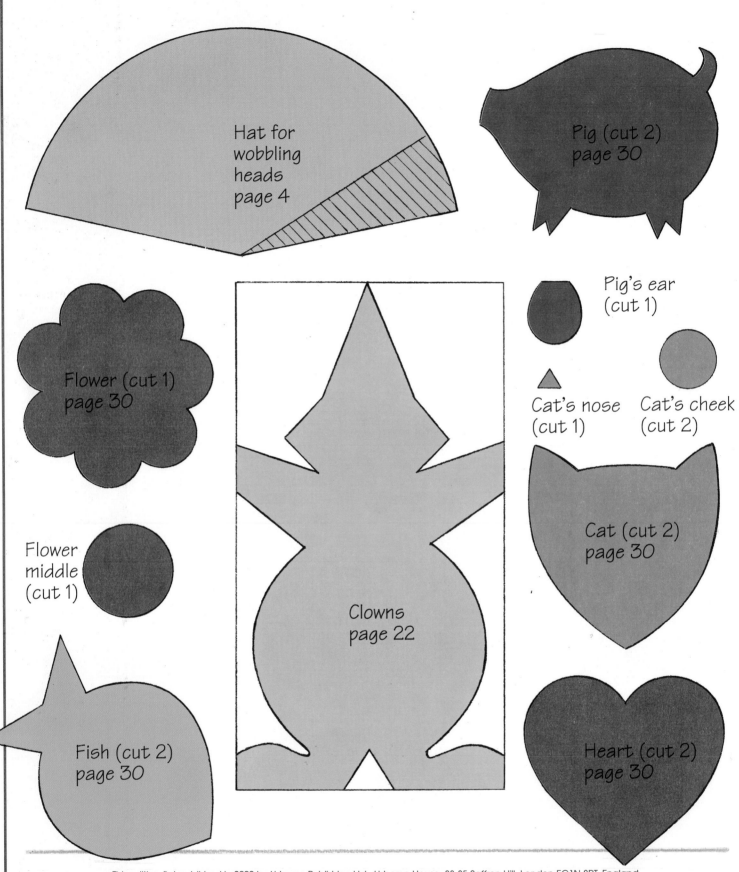

Hat for wobbling heads
page 4

Pig (cut 2)
page 30

Flower (cut 1)
page 30

Pig's ear (cut 1)

Cat's nose (cut 1)

Cat's cheek (cut 2)

Flower middle (cut 1)

Clowns
page 22

Cat (cut 2)
page 30

Fish (cut 2)
page 30

Heart (cut 2)
page 30